SURROUNDED BY HEADHUNTERS

The true story of Frank and Marie Drown, missionaries to the Jivaro (Shuar) Indians of Ecuador, South America.

By Sandra Klaus

Illustrated by Marvin Espe

CONTENTS

NOTE TO TEACHERS . . .

Before reading any of this book, we suggest you see "Pronunciation Guide" and "Counseling the Child Who Responds" on page 32. To get an overall view of the series, read through all five lessons prior to using the first lesson in class.

Practice reading the story out loud several times. Pronounce difficult words repeatedly until you feel comfortable with them. The better you know the story, the less you will have to read. Remember to maintain eye contact with your students, especially during times of invitation and challenge.

Before telling the story in front of your class, practice in front of a mirror or a live audience. Hold the book in front of you but do not cover your mouth—children need to hear you plainly. Check periodically to make sure that pictures are visible to your listeners.

Use one lesson per day. Briefly review story for newcomers each day. This can be done by showing one page at a time and asking children to tell about the picture. Or to save time, show only key pictures and quickly summarize for the group. Encourage children at the end of each story to return for the next session so they can hear the rest of the story.

Gospel Missionary Union is an interdenominational foreign mission society working in 20 countries. Evangelism, church planting and leadership training are at the core of GMU's varied ministries. GMU missionaries reach into different cultures ranging from primitive tribes to urban centers.

Published by: GOSPEL MISSIONARY UNION ■ 10000 N. Oak ■ Kansas City, Missouri 64155

ISBN 0-9617490-0-8   Printed in U.S.A.

SURROUNDED BY HEADHUNTERS

Lesson One

BIG PLANS/LOTS OF QUESTIONS

"What's the matter," Leon asked. "Are you afraid?"

"No," Frank insisted. He reached for the phone and began to dial. Halfway through, he banged the receiver back down. Turning to Leon he said, "I'm not afraid. Just smart. I'm smart enough to know Marie Page would never go out with a country boy like me." Frank paced the floor nervously as he talked. "Why she'd laugh in my face if I called her."

Leon wouldn't give up. "Frank Drown, you are a chicken. You've had your eye on her for a long time. This is your chance. A winter hayride through the snow. Why the whole senior class will be there." Leon picked up the phone and shoved it toward Frank. "Here, call her or I'll call her myself."

Reluctantly, Frank took the phone from his college roommate. "All right," he sighed. "But I already know what she'll say."

Frank slowly dialed the number to Marie's dormitory room. Rrring. Rrring. Frank listened as the phone rang once, twice, three times. After the sixth ring, he smiled with relief. "Well, that settles that. She's not home. You can't say I didn't try. Now, leave me alone."

Leon grabbed his coat. On his way out the door, he called to Frank. "You don't get off that easy. I'll go find her!"

"Leon, wait!" Frank couldn't believe Leon was actually doing this. But before he could catch him, Leon had disappeared into the cold, dark night.

Leon asked at the desk of each of the girls' dorms until he found out where Marie was. Quickly, he scribbled a note on a scrap of paper, signed Frank's name and sent it up to her.

The messenger pounded on the door. "Marie! Marie, are you in there?"

Marie's friend, Wanda, opened the door. "What's the matter?" she asked.

"There's a boy downstairs. He sent a note up to Marie. Frank Drown wants to invite her to the hayride tonight."

"Give me the note," Wanda said. "I'll give it to Marie."

"Wait!" The girl who'd brought the note stuck her foot in the door. "The boy's waiting downstairs for an answer. I'll take it down to him if you want."

"Marie, it's from Frank Drown. He wants you to go on the hayride with him. I told you he liked you, didn't I?"

Marie stretched out on the floor of the crowded little room. "Oh, Wanda, I'm tired," she said. "I worked all day at the dime store and I really don't want to go on a hayride. It's cold and wet and I don't have a snowsuit. Tell him I don't feel like it tonight."

This time it was Marie's friend who wouldn't give up. "Marie, you've been wanting him to ask you out. . . . I'll lend you my snowsuit." Hastily, Wanda scribbled something on the back of the note and handed it to the messenger to take back down to Leon.

Marie tried to intercept the note but the other girls were too quick. "What did you write on there?" she demanded.

"I told him you'd love to go and you'd be ready at 8:00." Wanda ducked. She could see Marie's green eyes flashing.

"You did what?" Marie shouted.

Wanda began searching frantically through her closet. "I told him you'd love to go and you'd be ready at 8:00. You haven't got much time. Here," she pulled out the bulky winter snowsuit and tossed it to Marie. "You'd better go get ready."

So, in spite of themselves, Frank Drown and Marie Page went on the hayride. They were both amazed at how much fun they had. Under the bright light of a full moon, Frank and Marie rode in the horse-drawn sleigh across the snowy field, sometimes singing with the rest of the group, sometimes rolling off the sleigh into a snowdrift and running to catch up again. The night went quickly and when he took her home, Frank asked if she would go out with him another time. Without even thinking about it, Marie said yes.

Before long, Frank and Marie were doing everything together. They went horseback riding and played tennis and they went hiking together. After graduation, Frank finally asked Marie to be his wife. Marie knew Frank was God's choice for her. They were married November 11, 1944 at Marie's church in Berkley, Michigan.

During the ceremony, Leon and Wanda glanced knowingly at each other as they stood at the altar with their friends. They were proud of themselves for their part in having brought Frank and Marie together.

But they weren't the only ones responsible for this marriage. God had planned it all. He had a special job for Frank and Marie to do. Even when they were children, God was already preparing them to be missionaries for Him. Let's see how. ➡

As a little girl, Marie attended Sunday school every week. She memorized Bible verses and heard many Bible stories. She even knew Jesus had died on the cross. But Marie had never accepted Jesus as her Savior.

One time, Marie's aunt and uncle took her to some special services at their church. At the end of one of those meetings, her uncle asked her if she wanted to "give her heart to the Lord Jesus."

Well, of course Marie said yes. And down the long church aisle she went to talk to the pastor. This made her feel good inside for a while. But then Marie heard that Jesus would return someday and take all who had accepted Him as their Savior with Him to Heaven. Marie began to be afraid. *Maybe when Jesus comes I'll be left behind,* she thought.

Marie wondered, *Did I really accept Jesus as my Savior that day or did I just do something because my uncle told me to?* Marie remembered a verse from the Bible that said if she would confess with her mouth the Lord Jesus and believe in her heart that God raised Him from the dead, she would be saved *(Romans 10:9).* Marie knew she believed Jesus had died on the cross and risen from the dead so she could have her sins forgiven. Now she felt like she wanted to confess—or to tell others—that Jesus was her Savior. So one day when she was 13, Marie stood before her church and told everyone that she knew Jesus as her Savior.

After high school, Marie went on to Bible college. She knew the Lord wanted her to be a missionary. She didn't care whether she was married or single, she just wanted to obey God. She would go wherever He wanted her to go and do whatever He wanted her to do.

Frank was so young when he accepted Jesus as his Savior that he doesn't remember exactly when it was. All he can remember is loving the Lord Jesus and wanting to please Him. But Frank was always sure of his salvation and never doubted at all that Jesus had died on the cross to take the punishment for his sin.

Frank went to Bible college planning to be a preacher in his home state of Iowa. But as he met missionaries at school and read more of God's Word, he realized that God wanted him to be a missionary, too. God gave him a new desire to tell people who had never even heard the name of Jesus how they could be saved.

After they were married, Frank and Marie prayed and asked God to show them exactly where He wanted them to go. While they waited, they did everything they could think of to get ready. They worked in their church. They went to a special school for missionaries. They were always busy talking about Jesus. And they even went to the mountains in northern California where there was a missionary "boot camp."

For over six months they lived at boot camp. Frank and Marie learned how to bake bread and repair engines—there wouldn't be any stores or repair shops where they were going. They learned a little about medicine, including how to give shots—there wouldn't be any doctors close by either. First they practiced giving shots to oranges. Then they had to practice giving shots of sterile water to each other. Learning to be a missionary was not always easy.

They learned how to survive in the wilderness. They did a lot of hiking and climbing and sleeping out of doors. One day about 20 young people from the camp climbed up Snow Mountain, one of the highest peaks in the area. A snowstorm stranded them at the top and they had to spend the night out on the windy, frozen mountainside.

Instead of being afraid though, Frank and Marie and the others built a big campfire and huddled around it. They prayed together and sang songs of praise to God. The young people took turns sharing favorite Bible verses and telling how good God had been to them in the past.

This was a dangerous time, but it was also good preparation for them as missionaries. Frank and Marie learned that God can be trusted to care for them in hard places. There would be even more difficult times on the mission field.

After camp, Frank and Marie continued to ask God where He wanted them to serve. One day at a meeting, they met Mr. G. Christian Weiss, the president of Gospel Missionary Union. Frank said to him, "We know God has called us to be missionaries. We want to work with people who have never heard about Jesus. Do you know of any tribe of Indians who know nothing about the Savior?"

Mr. Weiss's dark eyes danced with excitement. "Have you ever heard of the Jivaro Indians?" he asked. ➡

"They're a ferocious tribe of headhunters in the jungles of Ecuador. We desperately need another couple to work with them," Mr. Weiss said.

Frank was excited. "This is it," he said to Marie. "I know God wants us to go to the Jivaros." Marie nodded her head in agreement.

They studied everything they could find about the Jivaro Indians. They learned that these people worshiped evil spirits. The Indians talked with these spirits and depended on them for guidance and for healing. They knew absolutely nothing about God. In fact, these headhunters didn't even have a word in their language that meant God.

The Indians biggest fear was death. They believed that if they died they would spend forever in a place of punishment. They had no hope of ever going any place else. They had never heard of Heaven.

The Jivaros were murderers. They believed that no one ever died unless someone else had cursed them. So whenever there was a death, the family would ask the evil spirits to name the person who had cursed them. Then the family would go out in war parties to take revenge by killing that person and anyone else who got in their way.

The Jivaro Indians needed to hear about Jesus. Frank and Marie could hardly wait to go tell them.

As soon as they could, Frank and Marie said good-bye to their families and boarded a plane for the long flight to Ecuador. On the way there, many thoughts went through their minds. What would it be like in Ecuador, so far from family and friends? How would they be able to tell people who didn't even have a word for God about the living God who loved them and wanted them to be saved from their sins? If the people could not forgive each other, would they ever understand that God wanted to forgive them? And what would it be like to live in the jungle, surrounded by headhunters?

Frank and Marie didn't know the answers to these questions. But they did know that God had saved them and called them to do this work for Him. They would trust Him to care for them and give them the power to do what He asked.

What about you? Have you been saved from your sin? If you have, are you asking God to show you what He wants you to do? Are you willing to tell Him, like Frank and Marie did, that you will go anywhere He wants you to go and do anything He wants you to do? You can tell Him that right now in prayer. And you can trust Him just like the Drowns did.

But if you've never accepted Jesus as your Savior, the first thing God wants you to do is be saved. You can pray, too. Tell God you know you are a sinner—that you've done things wrong. Tell Him you believe Jesus died on the cross to take the punishment for your sins. You can ask the living Lord Jesus to be your Savior right now. Then after class, if you'll come and tell me that you accepted Jesus as your Savior today, I'll pray with you and show you some wonderful promises from God in the Bible.

What happened to Frank and Marie when they moved into their jungle home? You'll have to come back next time to hear the second part of their story, *(show front cover of book),* "Surrounded by Headhunters." ∎

Lesson Two

WILL THE KILLING EVER STOP?

"They're watching us again," Marie whispered to Frank. "What should I do?"

Frank continued to work at the little table he used for a desk. "Smile and keep on working," Frank said. "They're just curious. They want to see what we're doing."

Frank and Marie had finally moved into their home at the Macuma mission station in Ecuador. It was a sturdy house that Frank had built with the help of the Jivaro Indians. But it wasn't as "solid" as Marie had dreamed her first house would be.

The house was made out of bamboo, jungle vines and leaves. The walls had large gaping cracks in them and at almost any time of the day or night, Frank and Marie would notice beady black eyes staring in at them. The Jivaro Indians were fascinated by the way Frank and Marie lived. And they constantly stopped at their house to get a glimpse of what these "foreigners" were doing. Often they would look in the windows, but if they couldn't see enough through the windows, they would walk around the walls to peek through the cracks.

Frank and Marie learned much about the Jivaros. At first they seemed like friendly, outgoing children. But as they got to know them better, the Drowns discovered that many of the men were drunkards, wife-beaters and murderers.

And their habits were very hard to get used to. Because they didn't know any better, the Jivaros were dirty. They smelled of perspiration, smoke and rotten food. Most of the men and women wore their clothes until they were full of ugly stains. Instead of washing them, the Indians would just dye them a dark purple to cover the dirt. The Indians knew about soap, but they thought it was a medicine to be used only for skin diseases.

Still, God gave Frank and Marie a love for these people. They were willing to put up with anything to be able to tell the Jivaros about Jesus Christ, even letting them watch their every move through the cracks in their walls. Frank and Marie wanted so much to tell them how they could be changed and their lives could be filled with joy and peace, if only they would accept Jesus as their Savior from sin.

The missionaries at Macuma built a school and invited the boys from the neighboring village to come. Although some of the fathers didn't like the idea, 15 boys enrolled that first year. Many were smart and learned quickly. But they also had a hard time giving up their old ways.

On pretty days, the boys couldn't understand why they had to sit in the classroom. They were used to going hunting or fishing whenever they wanted to. The students were also given jobs to help pay their way through the school. One of those jobs was cutting weeds on the airstrip so the missionary plane could land to bring in the mail, medicines and other supplies. But Frank had as hard a time getting them to work outside as he did inside the classroom.

One day Frank and another missionary, Ernest Johnson, were clearing the airstrip by themselves. It was such a nice day the students had all taken off. As they worked, Frank heard a rustling in the jungle.

"Did you hear something?" Frank asked.

"Where?" Ernest stopped and looked around him.

Both men stood still, listening. "There," Frank pointed across the airstrip. "Do you hear it?"

Ernest nodded. "Sounds like someone's coming." ➤

Just then, one of their students, Chivia, stepped out of the jungle. He was wearing his new school clothes, but they were dirty and torn. "What happened to you?" Frank asked. "You're a mess!"

Ernest was a little more upset. "What have you been doing?" he demanded. "Look at your clothes!"

Chivia looked down and tried to brush the mud from his trousers. It was hopeless. There was nothing he could do. He lifted his hands, shrugged his shoulders and smiled innocently. With one front tooth missing from a fight he'd had, he looked like a little child.

Frank and Ernest couldn't stay angry. They just looked at each other and imitated Chivia's helpless shrug. The two men laughed loudly. Chivia fidgeted nervously. Frank put down his machete and carefully put his hand on the only clean place on Chivia's shoulder.

"Well, Chivia, what can we do for you today?" Frank asked teasingly. "We're already doing your work for you." He swept his arm around to show the many weeds they'd cut down that day. "Is there something else we can help you with?"

Chivia smiled again. Looking behind him, out to the hills, he said, "It's a good day for monkey hunting. I would like to go. Will you sell me some gunpowder?"

Ernest couldn't resist this chance to continue teasing Chivia. "Monkey hunting, eh? Going to come back with some good monkey meat? We haven't had monkey meat for a long time, have we Frank?"

Frank was enjoying the banter. "You know Ernest, I think that's a pretty good idea. Young Chivia here hasn't been able to help us clear the airstrip for some time now. Maybe he's been too weak to help us. I think what he needs is some good monkey meat to make him strong. I say we give him the gunpowder."

Ernest agreed, "I think so too." Pointing to a pile of dirt at the end of the runway, he said, "Why next week after Chivia becomes strong from eating his monkey meat, he'll level that pile of dirt for us in no time."

Frank led Chivia to the storage hut. "C'mon Chivia. How much gunpowder do you think you'll need?"

Chivia took the powder and disappeared into the jungle again. Nobody saw him for several days. School went on as usual without him.

One day as the other boys were sitting in class, a piercing scream came out of the jungle. They could just make out what the voice was saying. "Shuar maayi! Shuar maayi!" the Indians shouted.

"What is it?" Frank asked. He hadn't learned all of the Jivaro language yet. Ernest's wife, Jean, translated. "Men have killed," she whispered. Ernest ran out to talk to the Indians who had just come from the jungle. Later that evening, he told the story to Frank and Marie.

"Chivia didn't go monkey hunting after he bought that gunpowder from us last week. Instead he went straight to his uncle's house. Apparently his uncle had given his oldest daughter to be married to a young witch doctor. However, not long after she went to live with him, the girl got sick and died. The uncle thought the witch doctor had cursed her so he planned to kill him. He sent for Chivia and promised to give him his youngest daughter as a wife if Chivia would help him kill the witch doctor."

Marie was shocked. "Imagine, our Chivia who sang hymns so happily. How could he get involved in murdering anybody?"

Ernest went on. Frank and Marie listened intently. "Chivia and his uncle went to the witch doctor's house. They asked him to go fishing with them. He went, not suspecting a thing. After fishing for two or three days, they visited the house of another relative. They all sat down to drink." ➤

"When the witch doctor lifted the bowl to his lips, the uncle shot him in the stomach. He lay on the ground screaming in pain, but Chivia's uncle would not let anyone shoot him again. 'Let him suffer a while,' he said. Finally he motioned to Chivia who picked up a spear and drove it into the witch doctor's heart, killing him."

Frank and Marie could hardly believe their ears. "Where are Chivia and his uncle now?" they asked.

"Living with relatives near that same place," Ernest answered.

"Isn't somebody going to do something?" Marie exclaimed.

Ernest explained. "There isn't anybody who can do anything. The law is too far away." They talked about sending a letter to the army major in a nearby town, but Ernest reminded them there weren't enough soldiers to arrest all the Jivaros who had taken part in revenge killings. There was nothing they could do. But Chivia and his uncle wouldn't really go free. They would always be afraid that some member of the witch doctor's family would search for them and kill them.

"Isn't there any end to this killing?" Marie asked.

Frank sighed and said to the group, "The Jivaros will keep killing each other until no one is left. There is no hope for them at all—unless they believe in Jesus as their Savior. Then they can learn to forgive each other the way Jesus forgives."

That night, Frank and Marie prayed with Ernest and his wife. They were the only missionaries in thousands of square miles of Jivaro territory. How could they ever get the Jivaros to change their murdering ways? They felt helpless, but knew that God's power was able to save even these fierce Indians.

Frank and Marie decided that night they would not give up. They would continue teaching God's Word to the Indians—in the school and in Sunday services. They would take every opportunity to talk to the Jivaros about the love of God. They knew they couldn't force them to believe, so they trusted God to use His Word to change the Jivaros' hearts. Frank and Marie would just be faithful doing the job God had sent them to do.

Marie was shocked when she found out Chivia had been involved in a murder. Chivia seemed like such a nice young man. Marie could picture him sitting in class, listening intently and singing songs about God's love. He had learned how Jesus wanted to save him from his sin during some of the lessons at school.

Marie and the other missionaries thought Chivia was saved, but he wasn't. Chivia was still a sinner. He had just pretended to be interested in Jesus. We all know how to pretend to be something we're not, don't we?

The Bible says we are all sinners. Even though we haven't killed like Chivia did, everyone of us has done something wrong. In Romans 3:10, God says, "There is none righteous, no not one."

That means that no matter how good other people think you are, you can never be good enough to get to Heaven. But God's Word also says, "Believe on the Lord Jesus Christ and thou shalt be saved" (Acts 16:31). That means believe Jesus died on the cross to take the punishment for your sins and ask Him to forgive you and be your Savior. Do you believe on the Lord Jesus Christ? Would you like to tell Him that you do and ask Him to be your Savior? Then you come and talk to me as soon as our class is over. I'll be waiting for you over by the *(point out an easily identifiable object).* We'll pray together.

If you've already accepted Jesus as your Savior, you can be glad. Not only do you know your sins are forgiven and you will live in Heaven someday, but you also have God's promise to never leave you or forsake you before you get there *(Hebrews 13:5).* Just like Frank and Marie, you can trust God to do great things through you whenever you faithfully do the jobs He gives you. Think about a job you have coming up. Will you ask God to give you the power to do it well?

(Pause for prayer.)

What will happen to the Jivaros? Will they keep killing each other until none are left? Be sure to come back next time to hear more about them. And, we'll see what happens when Frank meets their deadly enemies, the Atshuaras. ∎

Lesson Three
HEADHUNTERS!

"What is it?" Frank asked. He handed the broken piece of clay to Ernest.

Ernest took the strange-looking pottery and rubbed it between his fingers, brushing the fresh dirt away. "Looks like Atshuaras," he said thoughtfully.

"Atshuaras?" Frank sounded amazed. "You mean the Indians that live south of here? What would their pottery be doing here?"

One of the Jivaro Indians working with Frank and Ernest explained. "Atshuaras used to live right here until our grandfathers drove them away. When the white men came and took the Jivaros' land, we moved inland to this place. We fought with the Atshuaras and forced them to leave. Now they live many days downstream, hidden deep in the forests like wild animals. It is impossible to get to them. And if you could, they would kill you."

The Jivaros told of wars between the two tribes. Although the Atshuaras didn't shrink enemy heads as the Jivaros did, they were hated and feared by all the Jivaros.

"Isn't there any way we can reach them?" Frank asked his Indian coworker. "Jesus died for the Atshuaras as much as He died for the Jivaros. They need to know God can forgive their sins, too." Frank and Ernest knew the power of the gospel could break down the walls of hatred and warfare that stood between these two tribes of Indians.

Their Indian coworker trembled at the thought of entering Atshuara territory. "No, no. There is no way. It is impossible." Before Frank could ask any more questions, the Indian ran off, afraid these missionaries would ask him to go with them on a journey he was sure could only mean death.

Frank looked at Ernest. "Someday . . . ," he said with a gleam of hope in his eye. "Someday, we will take the gospel to the Atshuaras. In the meantime, we will pray that God will make a way for us to meet them."

Frank prayed for the Atshuaras for several years after they found that first piece of pottery. Ernest and his wife had to leave the Macuma mission station, but Frank didn't give up. When a new missionary couple, Keith and Doris Austin came in, Frank told them about the Atshuaras.

Keith got excited about going to visit these Indians with Frank. They prayed for an opportunity to make the trip.

At last the day arrived. Frank and Keith convinced five Jivaros to take them into "no man's land", the area between the two tribes of Indians where neither Jivaro nor Atshuara was safe. They packed all of their gear—food, bedding, clothes and goods for trading—onto a cargo raft with a raised platform. Three Indians rode on the raft and two went with Frank and Keith in the dugout canoe.

The trip down the river was filled with surprises. One minute they would be gliding across deep quiet pools of water and the next, the pools would dissolve into white-water rapids swirling over the sharp rocks of the Macuma River. Every night, they built a fire and put some rice and beans on to cook. The Indians found leaves and poles and made shelters to cover the group as they slept. ➡

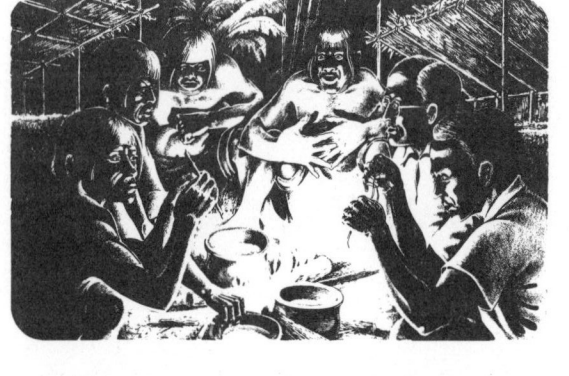

At night, they all sat around the fire, talking about the Atshuaras and some of the bitter wars that had gone on in the past. One Indian, Naicta, told about a headhunting expedition he had gone on into Atshuara territory to avenge the deaths of four Jivaros. They were close relatives of a man named Catani.

This is the story Naicta told:

"Just upstream from this spot where we are sitting, Catani took us to the house where his family had been killed. The house was empty but there were four mounds in the center of the dirt floor. The dead men were buried there.

"When we saw the graves, everyone went wild. All we could think of was killing. We hurried from house to house to challenge many warriors to join us. Soon we had about 100 men ready to go. Three of the men were witch doctors. Evil spirits appeared to them, telling them an Atshuara named Chiriapa had murdered the Jivaros. He was the one we should hunt down and kill.

"The next morning, we started down the trail. For two days we walked without seeing any houses. Again we consulted the evil spirits. Half of the men turned back, afraid to go on because the spirits said they would be killed if they went any further. We didn't mind their going back; we knew they had to do what the spirits told them.

"The rest of us went on. We traveled all night. Just before the sun came up, we came to a banana patch. The house was nearby. We snuffed out our torches.

"A rooster crowed, startling all of us. We made our plans. Catani whispered, 'Let's rush them. If you see a woman, capture her. If you see a man, shoot him. But don't shoot him in the head. We want that whole.'

"We surrounded the clearing and waited. Suddenly the dogs began to bark. We heard someone moving around inside the house. A deep voice shouted, 'Woman! Get up. Don't you hear the dogs? Our enemies must be outside.'

"We looked at each other in fear. *Chiriapa is at home all right,* we thought.

"The women made fun of him for thinking his enemies were after him. But Chiriapa shouted as though he knew we were just outside. He had been waiting for us to come ever since the murders. 'Listen, you head-shrinkers, I hear you! Come on, if you want to fight. I've killed many of your men. I'll kill you, too.'

"Again, his wives made fun of him. But now Chiriapa's only answer was the chilling sound of bullets clinking into place in his Winchester rifle. A shiver of fear ran through us as we heard that sound.

"We waited while the sun rose higher in the sky. As the day got brighter, Chiriapa got braver. 'Come,' he called to his wives. 'The cowards won't attack us now. It's daylight. Bring your baskets and we'll go to the river and fill them full of chonta fruit.'

"The heavy stockade gate creaked open. Out came women and children. We waited. Then came Chiriapa. The Jivaros fired the first shot. Chiriapa turned and ran screaming toward the house. 'Mura Shuaras!' he cried. 'They've come to kill me! They've come to k—.' Chiriapa fell in the doorway when a bullet tore into his back. The Jivaros swarmed around him and shot him over and over again. The women and children shrieked in fear.

"'Take his head!' shouted one of the witch doctors.

"The younger warriors stepped back. No one wanted to do it. Finally one of the old men pulled out a machete and slashed the neck, first on one side and then on the other. Taking hold of the long hair, he slung the head over his shoulder and started out the door. Everyone gasped as he turned around. The blood was dripping slowly down his back."*

Naicta continued his story. "We all followed him, taking the women and children captive. One woman got away. We knew she had run for help. Our enemies would be close behind us. We hurried as fast as we could. The witch doctor stopped once to carefully peel the skin off the head with his sharp knife. He threw the skull into the river and filled the head-skin with hot sand and small stones. He wanted to build a fire to cook it then, but we didn't dare stay in that place any longer. We knew the Atshuaras would catch us if we did. The witch doctor wrapped the head-skin in leaves, placed it carefully in a basket on his back and ran with us through the forest.

"When we arrived back at the Jivaro village, one of the witch doctors boiled the skin in a cooking pot filled with water, then laid it on a leaf to cool. He filled it with more hot sand and stones and boiled it some more. The process was long and involved. When it had shrunk to about one-third its original size, he rubbed charcoal into the face and neck and ears to make it extra black. A feast was prepared and for several days the Jivaros celebrated their victory over the Atshuaras."

Frank and Keith listened in horror. They went to bed that night wondering whether these Indians could ever understand God's love and forgiveness. Frank knew only the power of God could make them see their need to live together in peace.

Several more days of river travel brought them to a trading post run by an Indian named Taisha. Taisha was very careful not to take sides. He was a friend of the Atshuaras as well as the Jivaros.

After the usual long exchange of greetings, Frank and Keith explained to Taisha that they had come down the river as friends to bring him a message from God and that they wanted to take the same message to the Atshuaras. They wanted him to introduce them to the Atshuaras as friends.

Taisha seemed agreeable, but told them that all the Atshuaras he knew had been fighting among themselves recently and this would not be a good time to go. Frank and Keith were discouraged but wouldn't give up. They stayed with Taisha several days. While they were there many Jivaro Indians came to see them. Finally they met a Jivaro man who had married an Atshuara woman. They convinced him to take them to meet his wife's brother, an Atshuara named Timas.

"We won't go!" the Jivaros cried. One by one the Indians who had come with them backed out. Keith and Frank would have to go into Atshuara territory by themselves with this one Jivaro as their guide.

After traveling about six hours downstream, their guide whispered, "Tie the boat over there." At first Frank and Keith didn't know why they had stopped, but then they saw a barely noticeable trail. They stepped out of the boat and followed their guide.

After hiking about an hour along the jungle path, they came to a clearing. From the edge of the trees, they could look out and see a house. ➡

* Teacher: If children are very young, or if you feel description in this paragraph is too gorey, modify to fit your group.

"What do you think?" Frank asked. "It looks deserted. Should we try anyway?"

All of a sudden, out of nowhere, a high-pitched shout echoed through the clearing. "Don't come any further. Go back where you came from. We don't want any Jivaros or white men here!"

Their guide motioned for Frank and Keith to stay where they were. They watched as he walked bravely toward the house. This was his wife's brother's house. He must have felt safe.

The two white men stood alone. Keith looked around at the trees. There was no way of knowing who might be behind them. Finally he said, "I don't know about you, but I think I'd feel safer in there with him than out here alone."

Frank agreed. They approached the house cautiously. Inside they found one young Atshuara man with several women and children. Deadly silence filled the room.

"Where is Timas?" the guide asked the young Atshuara. At the same time he motioned Frank and Keith to sit down quietly. "Don't be afraid. These men haven't come to kill. They want to make friends with you. They've brought cloth and knives to sell. But more than that, they have come to tell you what the great creator-God has written in His Book. Send for Timas. Ask him to come back into the house and tell him to bring friends with him."

One of the women slipped out of the house. After a long time, she came back and whispered in the young man's ear. The young Indian looked more terrified than ever. "She brings a message from Timas," he said. "Timas will not see you. If you do not leave immediately, he will come back and kill these strangers."

Some of the other Indians in the house ran away in fear. Frank and Keith stood up, but their guide motioned for them to stand still. "Tell Timas we came to be friends," he repeated. "We do not want to hurt him."

Now Timas was angry. The message he sent this time warned, "Get those strangers out of my house. If you don't take them away at once, I will kill you all!"

Frank's heart was racing. He and Keith wanted to run for their lives. But they had to walk calmly away. If they looked afraid, they would make the Atshuaras think they had not come on a friendly mission. It took all their nerve, but they turned their backs on the house and the angry Atshuaras. They walked slowly back through the jungle to the Macuma river where they had left the canoe.

"I don't know," Keith sighed as they got into the canoe. "Do you think we'll ever get to the Atshuaras with God's Word?"

"Someday," Frank said. "But God will have to help us. I just thank Him for protecting us today."

Frank didn't know exactly how God had protected him that day until nearly a year later. Timas told the story to another Atshuara, who told the story to a Jivaro, who told the story to Frank. This is the story the Jivaro said Timas had told:

Timas was crouched in the brush beside the trail Keith and Frank had to walk as they left the house. Timas had made up his mind to kill the last man of the three to walk by.

First Timas watched the Indians run out. Then Keith walked by, followed by the guide. Frank Drown came last. Timas said, "I waited with my gun cocked. As I saw the men coming toward me I tensed my muscles. I pointed my gun at his head. But all of a sudden my arm went weak. My finger wouldn't move. I couldn't shoot even though I wanted to."

When he heard that story, Frank knew God had protected him. God had stopped the trigger finger of Timas that day on the Atshuara trail. Surely God did have a plan for reaching the Atshuaras. It would be dangerous, but he knew that the God who had protected him once could be trusted in every situation.

You can trust God, too. You can trust Him to save you from your sins. Remember the Bible says all have sinned. "All" includes you. God must punish your sin. The only way for you to escape the punishment is to have someone who has never sinned take your punishment for you. There is only one person who has never sinned. Do you know who it is? That's right, Jesus. Jesus took your punishment by dying on the cross. When He rose from the grave, it was proof that He had done everything He needed to do to save you.

The Bible says, "As many as received him, to them gave he power to become the children of God, even to them that believe in his name" *(John 1:12)*. Now it's up to you. Do you admit you're a sinner and do you believe Jesus died to take the punishment you deserved? If you do, God says He will forgive your sins and make you His child. You can pray right now and receive Jesus as your Savior.

Let's bow our heads. If you've already received the Lord, pray silently for your friends in class who need to be saved. If you've never received Jesus as your Savior and you want to do that today, you can pray this prayer with me. "Dear God *(pause)*. I know I am a sinner *(pause)*. I believe You died on the cross for my sins *(pause)*. Please forgive me and be my Savior *(pause)*. In Jesus' name I pray, Amen" *(pause)*.

If you prayed that for the first time today, will you raise your hand? *(Note any children who respond. Be sure to counsel them after class.)* Thank you. I want you to come see me after class. I want to show you that verse in the Bible so you'll never forget that you are God's child.

When you receive Jesus as your Savior, you can trust God to care for you even when He asks you to do hard things. Someday, He may ask you to be a missionary. Are you willing to trust and obey Him then? God may want you to tell your friend about Jesus today. Will you trust and obey Him now? Why don't you tell Him you will. We'll wait just a minute if you'd like to pray now. *(Pause briefly then close in prayer.)*

Frank and Marie and the other missionaries kept working with the Jivaros, but they wondered, *What will happen the next time we try to tell the Atshuaras about the true and living God? Will they try to kill us again?* Do you wonder the same thing? You'll have to come back for our next chapter in "Surrounded by Headhunters." ■

Lesson Four

CHIEF TSANTIACU—FRIEND OR FOE?

(Cover picture of Tsantiacu with paper as you read. Uncover where indicated.)

"I have radio traffic for Frank Drown. Is he there? Over." The radio crackled with excitement.

"He's right here. Over."

The voice on the radio blared the news. "I have a visitor—a very important visitor—who wants to talk with him. Over."

Frank couldn't stand the excitement. "Ask him who it is!" he begged the radio operator.

The voice at the other end wouldn't give him a clue. "I'll let him tell you himself," was the only response Frank got.

"Panchu!" an Indian's voice called over the radio. Panchu was the Indian name for Frank. Who could it be? Frank listened carefully. The voice didn't sound like any Jivaro he'd ever heard.

"Panchu," the voice repeated. "I am Tsantiacu, Atshuara chief."

Frank couldn't believe his ears. It had been years since they tried to contact the Atshuaras.

Chief Tsantiacu continued talking. "We have heard much about you," he said. "We want to be your friends. My people hope you will come to our country. They are waiting to see you. I invite you to stay at my house."

What an answer to prayer! After all these years of waiting and praying, here was an invitation from an Atshuara chief to come and even to stay in his house.

Roger and Barbara Youderian, another missionary couple who had come to Ecuador, had set up another mission station farther into the jungle. Tsantiacu had heard they had medicine and had come to investigate. Roger, or Roj, as everyone called him, explained they wanted to help the Indians by giving them God's Word along with the good medicines.

Roj and Tsantiacu made arrangements for Frank and some others to visit the Atshuara village. It would be a dangerous trip for the missionaries. Roj made the chief promise he would come personally with some of his men and go over the trail with them to be sure other Atshuaras didn't try to stop them.

Frank and his party got everything ready and waited for the chief. True to his word, Tsantiacu came. When Frank first saw the chief, he was impressed.

(Uncover picture of Tsantiacu.)

Tsantiacu looked confident and proud. His dark eyes were warm and friendly. His high cheekbones were streaked with paint. He wore no shirt, but a new striped "itipi" was wrapped around his hips, covering him from his waist to his ankles. His rifle seemed to be as much a part of him as his arms and legs. He was never without it.

Thick black bangs covered his forehead and his long hair hung down his back in a ponytail. His sideburns had never been trimmed and were tied in two more ponytails that stuck out, one on each side of his face. His head was decorated with bright red and yellow feathers from the toucan bird.

The group hiked several days through the dense jungle, climbing over fallen trees and squishing through swamps and mud holes. At last they arrived at a clearing. Stepping out from under the trees, Frank saw a huge house. It was about 40 feet wide and 90 feet long—the biggest Indian house he had ever seen. This was Tsantiacu's home.

Frank was anxious to begin telling these Atshuaras about God's love. Three times a day—morning, afternoon and evening—he called the people together to listen to the gospel message and to sing and worship God.

He began by telling them of the true God, the one who made heaven and the earth. Then he told them how God created all the animals, including the first man and woman. The people listened carefully.

Then Frank told them how God's Word, the Bible, says that the first man and woman sinned by disobeying God. He told them everyone since then had also sinned, even the Atshuaras. Frank explained that God's Son, the Lord Jesus Christ, loved them enough that He came to earth to die on the cross to take the punishment for their sins. The Atshuaras began to get restless.

But when Frank talked about how the Atshuaras could live forever in Heaven, the room became very quite. Everyone wanted to know how they could live forever.

Each time Frank finished preaching this message, Chief Tsantiacu would look at him and say with wonder, "Never have I heard such beautiful words. Tell them again." Frank preached until his voice was hoarse and his bones ached from sitting on the cramped bed-rack.

During their visit, Frank tried to learn the names of those living in Tsantiacu's house. The chief had three wives, one daughter and one young son. When he asked which wife was the mother of his children, Tsantiacu answered, "None. Their mother is dead. She was cursed. But the witch doctor that killed her is dead. I killed him." This was a good reminder to Frank and the others that even though these Indians were fascinated by the Bible stories, it would take a real miracle to change their murdering ways.

Before the missionaries left, Tsantiacu took them on a walk around his land. As they walked, they came to a clearing that was wide and straight, about a half mile long. Frank got excited. He knew with just a little extra work, this could easily be made into a landing strip for the missionary plane.

Frank explained his plan to the chief. Tsantiacu's smile told him he liked the idea. "Do you mean that if we made an airstrip here you would come to visit us and tell us more about God's Word?" the chief asked. Frank nodded. "Then that is what we want to do."

They walked off the dimensions of how wide and how long the airstrip should be and marked it by stripping branches from trees and sticking them into the ground.

The missionaries left with Tsantiacu's pledge of friendship and a warm invitation to come again. They promised to bring a doctor with them when they returned. At last, Frank felt sure they would be able to come and go as they had prayed in order to bring God's message to the Atshuaras.

When Frank returned to Macuma he told Marie about their visit. They planned more visits. And then the bad news came . . . war had broken out between the Atshuaras and the Jivaros.

There was no way for Frank to go into Atshuara territory now. It would be too dangerous. Their plans would have to wait.

After a long time the fighting slowed down. Frank couldn't wait any longer to go and visit Tsantiacu again. The missionary pilot flew in and picked up Frank and his group. This time they took along a doctor, just as promised.

As they circled over Tsantiacu's house to look at the new airstrip, the plane backfired. It would be a rough landing, but the pilot was sure they could make it. They bounced over the bumpy field, then the plane stopped.

Frank opened the door. "There's trouble," he said as he looked around outside the plane. There was not one Indian in sight and there was no sound except for the noise of the jungle. "Stay in the plane and be ready to take off again any second," Frank warned. Very cautiously, he began to walk toward Tsantiacu's house. ➡

Frank hadn't taken 20 steps when three Indians walked silently from the garden in front of the house. Tsantiacu was in the center. Two warriors at his sides. The chief's once friendly eyes were now cold with suspicion and anger. He waved his rifle with one hand and motioned Frank to go away with the other. There was no doubt about his message. He was telling Frank to get out!

But Frank kept walking toward them. He remembered he had a big white hat on. Thinking maybe they didn't recognize him, he slowly took it off. But it didn't matter. The warriors still threatened him.

Frank continued going forward, watching all the time from the corner of each eye for some movement in the jungle that would warn him of an ambush. He didn't see any. Frank remembered Roj and some of his missionary friends who had recently been killed by Indians in another part of the jungle. Their memory gave him courage.

Frank thought as he walked, *They were brave and willing to die in order to obey God's command to tell the Indians of God's love. I want the Atshuaras to hear God's Word. My life belongs to God. I am willing to die, too. I will serve God whether it means living or dying.*

Frank called out to the chief, "I come as your friend. I've brought a doctor just as I promised I would."

At the mention of a doctor, Tsantiacu relaxed a little, but still would not let Frank come near him. He was sure this was a Jivaro trick to catch him off guard. "If you come as a friend," Tsantiacu demanded, "why did you shoot at us from the sky?"

Shoot from the sky? Frank thought. And then he understood. The plane's backfire . . . to the Indians it sounded like gunfire.

Tsantiacu asked, "Why do you come in a different plane?" Frank had to explain to him that the other one had crashed in the jungle.

"Come see our new plane," Frank invited. After much reassurance, the missionaries finally convinced Tsantiacu they had come in peace. It wasn't long, then, until Frank was busy preaching God's Word again, three times a day. The Indians listened closely, begging for more whenever he stopped.

At the end of their visit, Tsantiacu put his arm around Frank's shoulders and said, "Panchu, I will never threaten you again as long as I live. Come back and tell us more about the Bible as soon as you can."

Frank returned often to visit the Atshuaras. One time when he went back, Tsantiacu tried to tell him how he was becoming like God's people. He explained that he and his warriors had gone on a killing raid. "But we did not kill anyone," the warrior chief said proudly. "You have taught us that God's Word says 'Do not kill.' So all we did was capture some of their women and bring them back in our canoes."

Frank wanted to laugh and cry at the same time. Wouldn't these Indians ever understand? How could he make them understand God hates all sin?

Another time, Tsantiacu was upset. "Panchu," he said to Frank. "I know God is powerful and I need His help. I hear my enemies are planning a raid to kill us. I have my gun ready. But you tell us God's people do not kill. If I am to defend myself, I must have God's help. I want to learn to pray."

Frank had a feeling the only reason Tsantiacu wanted to pray was to help him out of a tight situation. But they prayed anyway. Several months later, the chief told Frank how his enemies had started toward him, but then for no explained reason, had turned around halfway over the four-day trail. This seemed to convince Tsantiacu that God could answer prayer.

Months later, Frank visited the Atshuara chief again. After finishing a service at Tsantiacu's house one night and crawling into his bed-rack, Frank felt someone touch his arm. Turning, he saw the chief.

"Panchu," Tsantiacu said softly. "I need to bow the knee. I want God to forgive me the many evil things I have done. I want Him to give me power to overcome the devil." At last, Tsantiacu understood he was a sinner! Finally, he understood that only Jesus Christ could forgive him. ➡

Frank and Tsantiacu knelt together to pray. The chief talked to God, asking His forgiveness and help. While they were praying, Frank heard two other men praying with them.

When they finished, they found themselves surrounded by women. "Now Tsantiacu has become one of God's people," they cried happily. "He and his men have bowed their knees."

When Frank returned from that visit, he shared with Marie, "Now there are Atshuaras who are Christians. God has answered our prayers." That night they thanked God for Tsantiacu and the others who were saved. And they were glad they had not given up when things looked hard or even impossible, but that they had obeyed God and kept trying to reach the Atshuaras with the gospel.

It took Tsantiacu a long time before he really understood what he had to do to be saved. First he *listened* hard every time Frank talked about God and Jesus. But just listening to God's Word won't save you from your sin, will it?

Then Tsantiacu *acted* the way he knew God wanted him to. Remember he didn't go on killing raids anymore? But acting good won't save you either.

The chief even *prayed* to God when he needed God's help. It's true, God did help him, but even praying for God's help won't save you from your sins.

What did Tsantiacu have to do before he could be sure his sin was forgiven? Remember our Bible verse, "Believe on the Lord Jesus Christ and thou shalt be saved" *(Acts 16:31)*. Tsantiacu had to admit he was a sinner, then he had to believe that Jesus died on the cross, shedding His blood so that his sins could be forgiven. As soon as Tsantiacu did that he was saved.

Are you sure you have been saved? If not, and you'd like to be, you can show me you want to be saved by raising your hand right now. When I see you do that, I'll know you want to ask Jesus to forgive your sins. Then we'll go together to pray. You can tell God you know you are a sinner and want Jesus to save you, just like Tsantiacu did.

If you've already asked Jesus to be your Savior, you need to be willing to obey God, even when you feel afraid. It was hard for Frank to trust God when he thought Tsantiacu might kill him, but he obeyed God anyway. God promises He will never leave you nor forsake you *(Hebrews 13:5)*. He will be with you always, no matter how alone or afraid you feel. If you've already accepted Jesus as your Savior, you may want to pray right now. You can tell God you want to always obey Him and thank Him for His wonderful promise to be with you always.

(Allow short period of silent prayer, then close in prayer. BE SURE to follow-up on children who have raised their hands for salvation.)

After Tsantiacu was saved, he traveled among the Atshuaras to tell them God's message of love and forgiveness. Many other Atshuaras became Christians. But what about the Jivaros. Had any of them become Christians? And what will happen when these bitter enemies meet the next time. Will there be war or peace? Our next story will tell us. Be sure to be here for it. ■

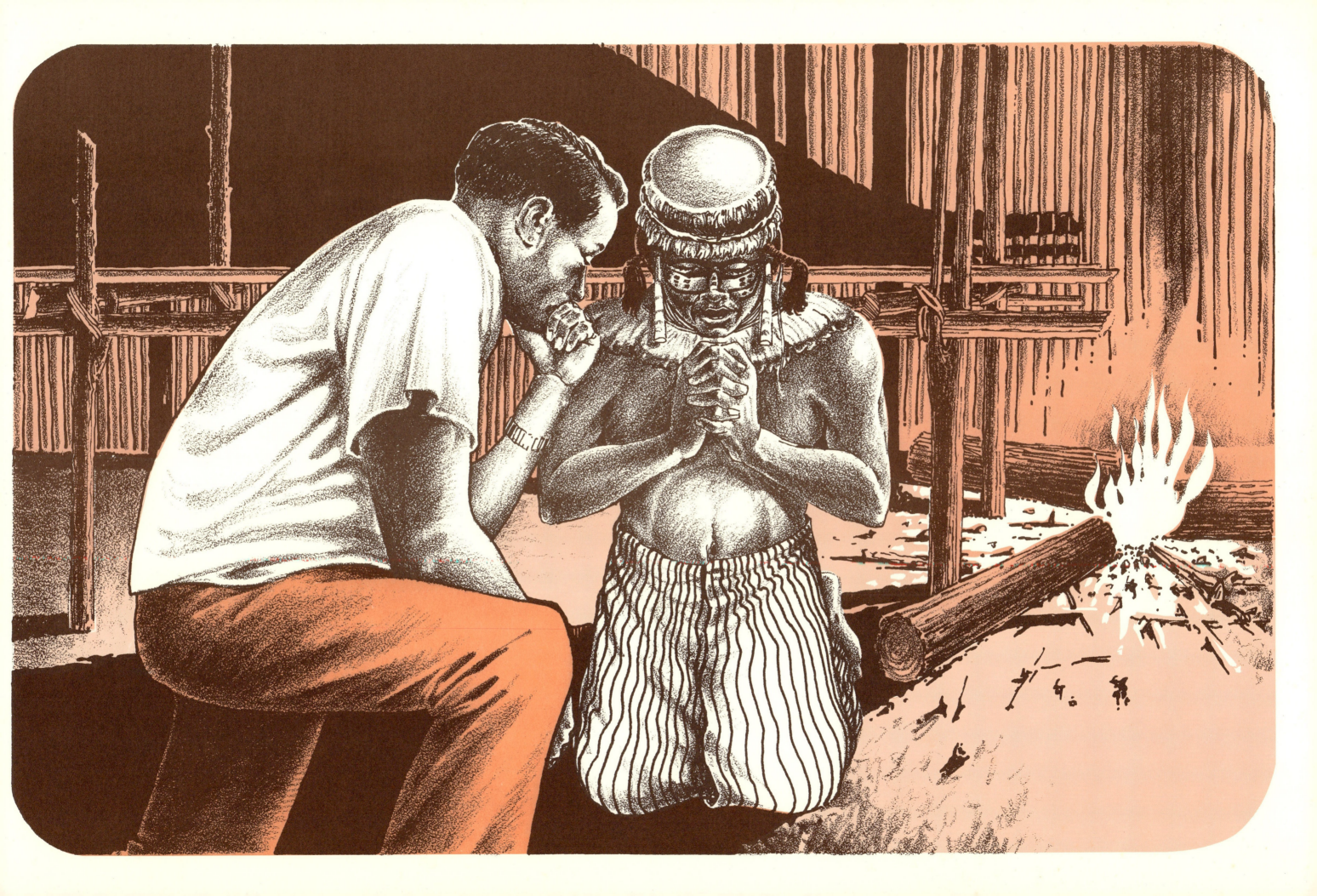

Lesson Five

PAKESH DOESN'T GIVE IN

"Oh, Mama, please," 12-year-old Pakesh begged. "Please won't you talk to Papa and tell him to let me go?" The little girl wanted this one thing more than anything she'd ever wanted in her whole life.

"No," her mother said as she pushed Pakesh away. "You heard him. School is for boys, not for girls. It will only make you lazy if you sit around reading the white man's words. Besides, you have already been promised to Tii as a bride. It won't be long until he comes to claim you. What good will school do you then?"

Pakesh stood frustrated in the center of the dirt floor of the bamboo house. "But Mama . . .," she pleaded.

Her mother bent over the fire in the center of the room, blowing gently on the hot coals to make them burn brighter. "You don't need to know how to read," she insisted. "You will soon be a Jivaro wife; you must learn to plant the garden so you can feed your husband; you must learn to build the fire to keep him warm; you must learn to cook his food and make the drinks that give him pleasure. Your father is right. School will make you lazy. Now get to work."

Pakesh obediently went to gather more wood for the fire. Her mind was rolling with thoughts as she tromped through the thick underbrush around her house. "My brothers go to the white man's school. They have told me about the God who loves everyone and about His Son who is much stronger than the spirits we know. Oh, how I would like to go there and learn more."

She found a dead tree which had fallen and began breaking off twigs and sticks. Pakesh thought about her future.

"My mother says I must stay home and learn to be a good Jivaro wife. But my father and mother are not happy. My father mistreats my mother. Long ago he bought a second wife and brought her to live here. When my mother cried about it, my father beat her. Now he has bought a third wife—one who is smaller than I am. And to pay for her, he has sold me to her brother, Tii. But I don't want to marry Tii. I want to go to the missionaries' school."

Pakesh headed back for the house. Her spindly arms were loaded with firewood. "I must convince my mother to let me go," she thought.

When the school for Jivaro girls started that year, Pakesh was there. What made her parents change their minds? It might have been the new clothes the missionaries offered to give the girls who came. Or it could have been that her parents would rather let the school feed her than have to work to feed her themselves. Whatever their reasons, God worked it out so Pakesh was in school and she was very happy to be there.

One Saturday she went home to visit her mother. She tried to tell her what it was like at the school. "It's wonderful," Pakesh said. "Besides learning to read and write, we have blankets to wrap up in at night instead of having to shiver by the fire. We have meals three times a day instead of just whenever there happens to be food around.

"And best of all," Pakesh said with a big smile, "at school we sing because we are happy. We're happy because we know about God and His Son, Jesus." Pakesh sang some of the songs for her mother. "See, Mama," she said. "These are happy songs. Our people don't have any happy songs. The witch doctor chants when treating the sick. The older men sing about killing their enemies. The women wail over the dead or dying. All our songs are sad. The missionaries' songs are so happy it makes me glad to hear them."

Pakesh's mother shook her head. "Nonsense," she said. "Your father was right. The white man's school is making you lazy. All you want to do is sit and sing your songs." Her mother grabbed her daughter by the shoulders and looked her squarely in the eyes. "Don't forget you are a Jivaro woman. Soon you will be a Jivaro wife. You will see there is nothing to sing happy songs about."

Pakesh returned to school with a gnawing fear growing within her. She knew it would not be long before Tii would come to take her to live with him. Tii was studying to be a witch doctor. Now that she knew about God and had accepted Jesus as her Savior, how could she possibly spend her life married to a man who called on evil spirits and worshiped them? Over and over again, Pakesh prayed that God would show her what to do.

In the meantime, her fear gave way to excitement. Pakesh's teachers, Panchu and his wife Marie, had spent much time explaining to her that becoming a Christian meant more than just saying the words of a prayer. Being a Christian meant she should obey God in all things.

One of the things God wanted her to do was confess, or tell about, Jesus Christ in front of her family and friends. Panchu taught what it meant to be baptized and planned a special baptismal service down by the river. Pakesh and four other students from the school were going to be baptized. They were the first Jivaros to become Christians since Frank and Marie had come to Ecuador. Everyone from miles around was coming to see this strange new ceremony.

Although none of the Jivaros watching understood what baptism meant, they had to admit that these believers had been freed from the fears of witchcraft and death and were happy in the Lord.

When the service was over, Frank and Marie prayed for all five new Christians. They knew it would not be easy for them to obey God when no one else around them did. ➤

Pakesh's struggles began almost immediately. A few days after she was baptized, the witch doctor Big Maantu and his son Tii came to visit her father. Pakesh knew this meant the time had come for her to prepare food and serve it to Tii. This would be the first step in the marriage ceremony. She hated the thought of becoming his wife. She knew God did not want her to be married to a man who did not believe in Jesus as Savior, especially not a man who was studying to be a witch doctor. What would she do?

When the time came, Pakesh carried the steaming bowl of food to where the men sat waiting. They all watched her and waited for her to hand the food to Tii. Pakesh paused and looked around. "I can't do it!" she said as she handed the bowl to her father. Everyone gasped. This was an insult to Tii and his whole family.

"You will!" her father insisted, shoving the bowl toward Pakesh.

"I can't, I can't," Pakesh cried.

Her father grabbed her and began to beat her with a big stick, trying to force her to go through with the marriage custom. Sobbing, Pakesh squirmed from his strong hands and ran outside. She hid for three days in the jungle, then ran through the trees to the house of one of the missionaries. "Help me," she cried as she pounded on the door. "Help me, please!" Pakesh pleaded.

The next morning Pakesh's father, who had been searching for her since she left, arrived at the mission station. "Where is my daughter?" he demanded. Frank and the others stood silently. "I know she is here. Send her out so I can teach her how a Jivaro woman should act!" the old Indian shouted.

Frank and Marie and the other missionaries refused to let him see his daughter. After storming around the mission station for a while, Pakesh's father marched back to his house.

Later in the day, Pakesh's mother came. She quietly asked to see her daughter. Thinking it was safe, the missionaries called for Pakesh. Pakesh agreed to go home with her.

Frank and Marie watched as they walked away from the mission station. But Marie cried when she saw Pakesh's father appear from the jungle. Instead of heading for their home, Pakesh's mother grabbed her daughter's arm and dragged her down the trail toward the river. Her father pushed her until they entered a canoe and crossed the river to Tii's house. Pakesh's parents had tricked her and the missionaries.

On the other side of the river, her father pulled her out of the canoe and shoved her along the path to Tii's house. Just as they stepped into the clearing, Pakesh broke loose and ran away again. No one saw her for three weeks. She was gone so long everyone believed she had died in the jungle. Tii was angry.

Frank and Marie were sad. They were sorry that Pakesh had to suffer because she was trying to be obedient to God. One night they were with the other missionaries in their house, talking about Pakesh's courage. They all prayed that because Pakesh had been obedient, other Jivaro Indians would want to know Jesus as their Savior.

"Shh! . . . Listen," Marie whispered.

Nobody moved. They all strained to hear a sound. "There it is again," Marie said. "I think there's someone outside." Marie cautiously opened the door and peered out. "Pakesh!" she cried.

Frank rushed out and scooped up the poor girl. She was ragged and thin. She was weak from hunger, but still confident that God would keep her from becoming a witch doctor's wife.

Frank and Marie fed her and gave her a warm place to sleep. The next day, they explained to her how God had answered their prayers. Tii had been so insulted when she ran away the second time, he refused to have anything to do with her. He didn't want to marry her any more.

Because Tii refused to marry her, Pakesh's father eventually let her live quietly at home again and even let her return to school.

Pakesh found out that being a Christian is not always easy. She was beaten and had to hide from her family and neighbors because she refused to do what she knew was wrong. The other young people from the school who had accepted Jesus and been baptized had the same kind of problems.

And the Jivaro Indians watched all that was going on. As they watched, they saw that Pakesh and the others were serious about their faith. Their new faith had changed them. They were no longer afraid to die. They saw that Pakesh's God was a powerful God who could keep her safe even when the witch doctor was angry with her. And they began to ask Frank and Marie more questions about how they could believe in Pakesh's God.

Soon, many more Jivaros began to attend the preaching services Frank held in the boys' school. Many more heard how they could be saved from their sin. Soon there were many Jivaro believers. Even Pakesh's brothers and mother and father eventually became Christians.

Frank and Marie decided it was time to build a separate building for church services. The new Christian Jivaros all helped to build the bamboo building. They named it "God's House." ➡

Throughout the jungle, the Jivaros spread the word that there was a new kind of house in Macuma. "No one eats or sleeps there," the Christian Indians would say. "When we gather together we do not talk of war and witch doctors' curses. We pray to God and listen to His Word. No one needs to be afraid to enter God's House," they said with pride. "We want everyone to come and learn with us."

And come they did. Sometimes there were more than 100 people worshiping together. One day, even Chief Tsantiacu and the Atshuara Christians came to visit God's House. The Jivaros and the Atshuaras, once bitter enemies, sat down in peace and worshiped the living God, the one who had sent His Son to be their Savior. What a miracle God had worked among these people.

Today there are many schools and churches in the jungle where there had been such fierce killings and warfare. The Jivaros and Atshuaras don't go on killing raids anymore when someone dies. The Indians now live in peace.

Frank and Marie Drown are not in Ecuador anymore. But God is. He is still changing people there. As the young people from the mission schools graduate, they are becoming preachers and teachers who tell their own people how Jesus wants to be their Savior and give them new lives—forgiven of sin and ready for Heaven.

Isn't God wonderful? He is able to change ferocious headhunters into preachers and teachers who share the gospel of peace.

God is able to forgive all sin. He is able because Jesus died on the cross and took the punishment for all sin. That includes the sins you have done. These Indians were murderers. Murder is a terrible sin. But fighting with your sister or brother or friend is also sin. Talking back to your parents is sin. Doing something your teacher tells you not to do is sin.

God promises to forgive your sin if you will believe Jesus died on the cross to take your punishment. John 3:16 says, "For God so loved the world, that he gave his only begotten Son, that whosoever believeth in him should not perish, but have everlasting life."

Let's all bow our heads. Three days after they took His body off the cross and laid it in the grave, Jesus came back to life. He is alive in Heaven today. He loves you and wants you to receive Him as your Savior. Would you like to do that today? If you raise your hand, I'll know you want to and we'll pray together. Is there anyone here who wants to receive **Jesus as Savior?** (*Pause for response. Give instructions for children who raise hands to meet with you at a specific place and time for counseling.*)

All right, you can look back up at me. Some of you have already accepted Jesus as your Savior. Have you decided to obey God in everything you do? Are you willing to do what He asks, even if it means you have to suffer? You probably won't be beaten like Pakesh was. But when you try to obey God, your friends may make fun of you.

Your friends may want you to steal something. You know that's wrong. If you obey God and tell them no, they may call you a coward or make fun of you. What should you do? (*Let children respond.*) Will it be easy? No. But God says He will help you. The Bible says, "I can do all things through Christ, who strengthens me" (*Philippians 4:13*). Ask God to help you obey Him—even when it's hard. ■

PRONUNCIATION GUIDE

Atshuara *(aht-'shwah-rah)* Indian tribe living in southeastern Ecuador, speaking a dialect of Jivaro; enemies of the Jivaros.

Big Maantu *('mahn-doo)* witch doctor living across the river from the Macuma mission station.

Catani *(cah-'tah-nee)* Jivaro chief and witch doctor.

Chiriapa *(chee-ree-'ah-pah)* Atshuara whose head was taken and shrunk by Jivaros on a killing raid.

Chivia *('chee-vee-ah)* schoolboy who deceived missionaries for some gunpowder.

itipi *(ee-'tee-pee)* wrap-around skirt worn by Indian men.

Jivaro *('hee-vah-roh)* tribe of Indians living in eastern Ecuador; enemies of the Atshuaras; Jivaro is Spanish name for them; they call themselves Shuar.

Macuma *(mah-'coo-mah)* jungle mission station on the banks of Macuma River; later base for other mission outstations.

Naicta *('nah-eec-tah)* Jivaro who related story of head-hunt he participated in.

Pakesh *(pah-'kish)* one of the first Jivaro girls to be baptized.

Panchu *('pan-choo)* name given Frank Drown by the Jivaros.

Shuar *('shwar)* literally means "people"; Indians preferred this name to Jivaro which meant "savage."

Tii *('tee)* a Jivaro Indian name.

Timas *(tee-'myas)* hostile Atshuara chief who planned to kill missionaries.

Tsantiacu *('tsahn-dyah-coo)* Atshuara chief who welcomed missionaries.

COUNSELING THE CHILD WHO RESPONDS

Both an invitation for salvation and a challenge for Christian growth are included in each of these lessons. It is best not to pause or separate the invitation from the story text, as some children will begin to "tune you out" the minute they think the story is finished. The invitation is presented in several formats. If you are uncomfortable with any, plan to give the invitation in your own words.

Be sensitive to the child who responds. Do not assume that because the child raised his hand or met you in a certain location that he is ready to make a decision for Christ. Carefully question him. Ask, "Why did you raise your hand today?" Not, "You wanted to received Jesus as your Savior, right?" Avoid questions that can be answered with a simple yes or no.

Once you have determined the child truly wants to receive Christ as Savior, counsel him on his level. Do not overwhelm him with Bible references. It is usually best to focus on one verse which gives both the condition and promise of salvation (Romans 10:9, Acts 16:31, John 1:12 or John 3:16). Use the verse from that day's story.

Since you cannot know the child's heart, do not give him false assurance of salvation. Let the child receive assurance from the Holy Spirit through God's Word. Rather than telling the child "Now you are saved!" Ask the child to read the verse again. Then ask the child what the verse says you must do in order to be saved. Ask the child whether he has done that. Ask the child if he is saved. Write the verse reference down for the child to use as a basis for his salvation.

For additional helps in leading a child to Christ, write Child Evangelism Fellowship Press, Box 348, Warrenton, MO 63383. Several excellent helps are available including a video training series, and a self-study workbook with a cassette recording of counseling sessions.

BACKGROUND INFORMATION

The two tribes of Indians in these stories are referred to as Jivaro and Atshuara. However, from a linguistic viewpoint, the term Jivaro (Shuar) could be used to describe both groups. Although the stories are true, names have been changed in some cases.

In 1896, Gospel Missionary Union (working under the name of The World's Gospel Union), was the first evangelical mission allowed to enter Ecuador. Since then, a field headquarters has been established in the capital city of Quito. From there, GMU workers have reached into all three geographical areas of the country: the coastal lowlands, the Andean highlands (Quichua Indians) and the eastern jungle area called the Oriente, where the Shuar (Jivaro) Indians live.

There was no written language among the Quichua or Shuar Indians when GMU began to minister to them. Missionaries tackled the demanding process of learning the language and developing an alphabet. Today the Quichuas and Shuaras both have the complete New Testament in their languages. GMU translation teams, working closely with nationals from both tribes, are in the process of completing work on the Old Testament.

GMU-related churches join together to form the largest evangelical church association in Ecuador. There are presently 422 GMU churches and congregations involving over 60,000 Christians in this small country.

Radio programs are used to take the gospel into areas missionaries have been unable to reach. Three GMU radio stations, now owned and operated by nationals, broadcast daily in the Spanish, Shuar and Quichua language.

GMU has specific mission projects in Ecuador that need financial support. We welcome your group's participation in this ministry. Write to the Director of Development for details on how you can be involved in ministering to the Shuar.

Gospel Missionary Union
10000 North Oak
Kansas City, MO 64155
(816) 734-8500

2121 Henderson Hwy.
Winnipeg, Manitoba R2G 1P8
(204) 338-7831

Frank and Marie Drown are currently serving as northcentral representatives for GMU and are available for mission conferences. Write to them in care of Gospel Missionary Union, 10000 North Oak, Kansas City, MO 64155.